# WEEPING IN WORDS

Mohammed Adil

Copyright © Mohammed Adil, 2017.

## All Rights Reserved.

Nopart of this publication may be reproduced or transmitted in
any forms or any means, mechanical or electronic or photocopying and recording, or by any information storage and retrieval system, without permission in writing from the author, except in the case of certain non-commercial uses permitted by
copyright law.

Requests for permission for or further information on usage of this document should be addressed to: adilspoetry@gmail.com

# WEEPING IN WORDS

If cursed by fate are those

who cry in tears;

then blessed by this mind I am,

who weeps in words.

WEEPING IN WORDS

*Book designed and written by*
**Mohammed Adil**

*Also by Mohammed Adil*

**Why POETS NEVER SLEEP:**
**Poems and parables**

Mohammed Adil

Brace yourself, my diary.
Brace yourself, my pen.
Here comes the night
and to it, shall I vent.

# WEEPING IN WORDS

Mohammed Adil

**WEEPING IN WORDS**

Mohammed Adil

Only when you stop
aiming for the sky
and chasing distant stars,
can you learn
to cherish the sweet grass
'neath your feet.

Ego can enflame

your mind and

heart

to fine ashes

before you even get a chance

to wonder

where it was

that you started spilling

the gasoline.

Mohammed Adil

*Prejudice*

Their discriminated skin bled
by the brutal lashes
on their bare black backs,
soaked in sweat
as they worked in the rich fields
burning in the hot sun.

Every whip to the slave,
peeled his skin a little.
Every whip by the master,
thrilled him a little.

And so he lashed
harder
and harder
until the nigger's sore throat
ceased to scream
and his exhausted lungs

gave up on his struggling soul.

Let us not forget
what used to happen.
Let us not underestimate
our evil, within.

Mohammed Adil

Some mistakes are too big
for you to forgive yourself

and there is nothing worse
than the bitter sting of regret.

## *Murderer Of Mama Bird*

There was a bird named curiosity.
When I was younger, I often used to
injure her wings for fun,
but she always healed
within no time and would fly again.
As I grew older, I grew desperate and
wanted to test
the horizons of her healing
and so one day, I caught her
while she
flapped her wings as hard as she could
to escape my clutches.
I, then, opened her breast
while she screamed
and sunk my fingers into
her bloody chest and
pulled out her heart and ate it.
The feathers in the air

## Mohammed Adil

settled on the ground

and the bird never healed again.

Little did I know,

she had laid eggs before she died.

Today that I'm a man,

her grown children have found me.

They dig their beaks

into my brain and

peck into my chest.

They have

ripped out my vocal chords and

my tongue

so no one can hear me cry.

They feed off me

little by little each day

leaving only my heart,

my eyes

and my fingers safe,

so that I can write

my suffering,

then re-read my own cries

written

in a dark blend

of blood

and blue ink

while people

applaud.

## To Be Heard

I've been looking
for guns and pocket knives to
make people
pay attention
to what I say
but I'm too broke to
afford them.

But I've learned that
curse words and
rhymes can do just
the same,
for much less.

## WEEPING IN WORDS

Guns and nooses

are tools for losers.

If you have a spine,

write poetry.

Take pride in your bruises.

Mohammed Adil

***Writing***

aor amillionthoughts ,
a million times
these tired fingers dive
and sink
into the weary typewriters.
But we don't mind
for the pain in the chest is far greater.
Amillionthoughts
swim desperately
through the typed pages
as they fear drowing alone,
without being read.
don't mind But we
for the pain in the chest
is far too protruding
to be concealed by these aching fingers.

***Fireworks and Cigarettes***

Some light fireworks.
Some light cigarettes.
The dead spoke vital words
and the world claims,
it never forgets. But I
know it does. On
this,
my heart bets.

The inability to express
the thoughts my mind weaves
and the secrets my heart,
thus, has to keep
could be the reason why
poets never sleep.
The sorrow remains unshared.

The suffering never off-sets. So while some light fireworks, some light cigarettes.

## *Dying And Sickness*

Nine days, bedrid. Cold
sweat , can't shit. Neon
green, hot piss.
Lips quiver, crave dead wife's kiss.

Last walk with her, never ambled.
Now all hair, shambled.
Last penny, gambled.
Money, robbed. Market-
grocery, snaffled.
All across the country, family- scrambled.
No tragedy, can anymore-baffle.
Only fantasy, scaffold.

Mohammed Adil

**Wackadoos Of The World**

Cursed with pessimistic eyes
and cynical minds,
we see the world and can't help
but weep at times.

We see our future,
our fate-
far from bright.
Maybe that is why
they call us fanatics
and exiles,
because we know
how to live with no hope,
how to live in no light.

### *Rodent On The Road*

Tonight,

I drove my bike

over a rodent

of the size of a small cat.

As I ignored it

and drove further,

leaving blood trials behind, I

couldn't help

but pull the brakes

and turn back to look at it.

It was no more

than a few seconds

since I had killed the animal

and it was already

being feasted on by a dog.

This left me thinking

Mohammed Adil

if I should be

feeling guilty for killing

or boastful about

feeding the hungry?

***Always me***

This hall is filled
with the chatter of the party,
people enjoying food,
and the drinks, blurry
faces flirting
with other blurry faces

and suddenly, while me
and my friends are engaged
in a conversation,
I find myself,
slowly being engulfed
by a smoke rising from
beneath my feet and I
hear their
and everyone else's voice
fade into thin air

Mohammed Adil

as I feel

a cloud of misery

taking over me.

Why me?

Always me.

Mistook her for an angel,

when she was a snake

that firsts,

poisons your insides;

then later,

bites its way out

through your skin.

***If Painful, Perhaps True***

We test the loyalty of the ones we love
>by hurting them the most,
>>forgetting how deceiving
>>>and unworthy,
>>>>we,
>>>>>ourselves,
>>>>>>can be.

### *People And Butterflies*

People will leave
and you will too.

Who you thought were butterflies
will turn out moths.

The fingers that glided down your cheek
will try and strangle you.

You will find yourself amidst nothing
but blankness of uncertainty.

This is when you need to stop trying,
sit back,
let a few mistakes nearly kill you
before you learn,
how to live

all over again.

### *Time Tells Tales*

How swiftly the good years fly.
How quickly our clock strikes.
How easily we fall in love.
How subtly our stars align.

And as we part,
oh, how the dormant night
mourns and cries;
how those heavy tears
hang from our chins and shine.
How our loved ones, grow with us and die.
Look,
how quickly our clock strikes.
Oh,
how swiftly the good years fly.

## WEEPING IN WORDS

I know,
you're caught up in the middle
being eaten up by life, little by little,
having your confidence crippled,
and your fade fiddled.

I know,
you're caught up in the middle.
But you too have teeth and must
try to fight back and nibble
for you are no less to take on a quibble.

And may I remind you
to not take this page to
be some scribble
because you know
how you're caught up in the middle.

## *The Gift Of Free Will*

Do not let
yourself be
the paint stains
on yesterday's canvas.

You are a clean slate
each morning
and you are your chalk
and your stone.
It is up to you
to either
write a beautiful day
or carve heartbreaks
onto yourself.

### *Spirits, Stronger Than Bones*

Break your heart
against other hearts.
Let your ears bleed
from their mockery.
Fall a hundred times
even if
there is only a little chance of walking.
Get kicked out places.
Be disgraced by everyone

and I give you my word.
You will be beautifully surprised
by how much you can take
and still remain
in one piece.

## *The Longer You Ache*

The more

a bow is bent,

the better it shoots;

but never be consumed

by the greed

of the arrow's speed

because every bow breaks if

stretched too much

and holds

no use

for anyone

thereafter.

### *Rain And Sad Songs*

Every mood has its minutes
and every poem has its purpose.

Every creature cries from the nets.
For every sin, we owe a pound of flesh.

Every sun has its sets
and every night leaves you restless.

Every rainbow is a gift from the storm after
every raindrop has sung its sad song.

Every door opens to a new road
as every mystery waits to be explored.

For every pain that ceases to be hidden,
every poem begs to be written.

Mohammed Adil

For everyone that the war has killed,
every grave must unwillingly be filled.

***Visitors***

When t hey leave
with their packed bags and
I'm left home-alone, once
again,
 this aching chest
 andthis lonely heart
will eat me  alive .

Mohammed Adil

## *Unturned Calendars*

I haven't showered

or shaved in days.

Not that I like bearing this image

of myself,

but I really

wouldn't mind if the maggots

start burying their homes in me

today.

### *Haunted Me*

Dusty fans hanging loose from the ceiling;
creaky stairs, bordering on crumbling; empty
halls; echoing walls-
aging with the cob webs;
dried and rusty faucets.

The abandoned house is an allegory
for my heart
that waits for someone to claim it
before it collapses into the clutches
of my own self-destructive mind.

Mohammed Adil

***Premonitions And Dreams***

Only when
I spit out my teeth into the sink,
grab and uproot
most of my hair from the scalp,
cough up pieces of my dry lungs
onto the bathroom floor
does the guilt of a hundred cigarettes
finally weigh in,
leaving me
weeping without tears
and vomiting vacuum.

### Hollow

I'm filled with shadows inside me
that have never seen light,
waiting desperately for when
I'll set them free.
But I don't let them out
and keep them locked and
caged within me.

Better be filled with shadows
than be empty.

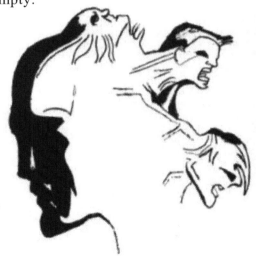

***Self-loathing***

   The bathroom sink
      overflows
and I don't understand
    why I'm disgusted by
   the same water
that just washed me.

## *Hymn From A Sinner's Grave*

Eyes tight closed.
Spiders nesting inside my throat.

Half skin gnawed by bugs.
Half lungs filled with dust.

The cob-webs in my neck
absorb the sounds and turn
the screams silent.

Soundless like rocks,
motionless like tress,
uglier than moths,
flesh, eaten by fleas;

I can't help but envy
when I hear the people above speak
words deeper than sea

and their throats that remain so free,

free from spiders
that feed
on voice,
free from dust
that leaves me
no choice.

## *No One Else, If Not You*

A famer was frightened
when he heard
that the landlord
was ceasing away the land
from other peasant farmers
as the fields
were the only source
of his income.
He thought it was unjust
for the landlord to get
all of his hard-gown
crops
and so
he burned down
all of his yield.

Later, that evening,
he found out that

the landlord, ceasing property,
was all just a
rumour.

The next time
you feel threatened,
just continue
to water your crops,
but always have some
kerosene ready.

### *Monarchy Of The Morning*

When the world stays safe
in its silent slumber,
my sleepless heart can't help but
miss and remember
the monarchy of the morning,
when the early birds
beat their wings against the cold winds
while they tweet their
way through the blinding fog, declaring
their reign over the daylight as the
hooting owls finally descend from their
nocturnal thrones.

Mohammed Adil

***Like The First Day Of School***

Sometimes,
I get very nervous
and scared before leaving my house.
The faces I see daily
begin to look strange
and make me feel like an alien
when I'm surrounded by them.

It is at times like these that
I have a wake up call
to remind myself how everyone is
a stranger to everyone else and
there is no one that truly
understands what we really feel
except for ourselves.

### *The Agony In My Legs*

Restlessness runs in the bones of my thighs.

The warmth, my lap longs to provide

has been rejected

and made fun of

many a times.

Numbness runs in the bones of my feet.

Alone, for too long now,

they've been walking.

Mohammed Adil

***Security From Vulnerability***

I walked a silent street at midnight

with immense sorrow

and incarcerated remorse

sprouting out

from my aching chest.

It was when the orange rays

of the bright streetlights

embraced me

that my eyeballs

were drowning

in tears and even though

the lights

were supposed to expose my

teary eyes to the world

there was no one there to witness it.

And I must admit,

there is a bliss in sobbing alone

sometimes.

There is a safety

from pretentious sympathy ;

a security

in this beautiful invisibility.

*False Hopes*

In the end,
we always wind up
thinking about the beginning.

It is as if
something is
asking us
to stop leaving
and stay.
The flashbacks fighting
against the fast lanes,
memories
keeping us from being delusional
about a delightful future,
just to stop us
from moving forward
and just stay.

Something always makes it difficult

to move on

and it is about that time

that we give it a chance

and not be mesmerized by

a better future

that is un-promised,

and prevent

what we already have now

from becoming

worse.

Mohammed Adil

***Another Night***

Underneath the starry night sky,
I swing in the hammock of nostalgia,
dangling back and forth
between forgotten memories
that have collected dust in my mind
over the past few years.

And oh, how I miss that rain,
the smell of the wet walls
and sliding down the stair railing.

This hammock holds an essence,
so warm, so blissful
that it is saddening.

***Paws***

My cousin

carries his kitten

everywhere he travels. He

carries him inside his

bag pack to avoid a fuss in trains and

busses. When I asked him why it was

so necessary

to  carry the cat

everywhere

he went.

He said that the kitten

keeps him from being lonely.

And this tells me a lot about

how far we can go

just to keep loneliness at bay.

Mohammed Adil

***Pain In The Puns***

When my jokes are at their finest
and sarcasm, on point,
does the bitter realization strikes,
making me wonder
if they truly understand me
and the broken mess that I foster beneath
as I continue to throw banters
from the debris of my mistakes
and rubble of my remorse while
I make them laugh
to their tears,
denying myself,
my own.

## *Cynic's Suicide*

Arms that envelope you,
can abandon you.
The bed that braced you
will leave you desiring for an
other body beside you.
The cold mornings you wake up to,
will make you want to end your life
then and there.


The couples on the park benches
and the audacity of that sight will
make you smile
and realize how
luxurious and scarce love is,
for you.
The person you dream about
will dwell in your fantasies forever
as you find loneliness

more latching than love,

a noose less damaging

and death more meaningful

than life.

More ears than mouths.
Yet,
they don't listen.

More tongue-noises
than heart-voices
as they choose to keep
their fertile brains barren.

With high functioning
and judgmental minds,
loud mouths and numb ears,
where are we headed?

I am a fugitive of the largest genocide.
An escapee, an eeile.

I am the one spirit,
your society failed
to kill.

Mohammed Adil

eot all dreams come true.

sost tust remain fantasies.

I have never known responsibility. I
have never followed discipline.
I have never tasted passion and ambition.
But I have found purpose
and this is mine.

Every morning
I see people,
ten years older than me,
carrying their
heavy bags,
leaving for work
but have accomplished nothing
for themselves
and it makes me feel
like I have achieved more than them
in all the time I had.
Maybe one day,
I'll have to face the gnashing teeth

of responsibility too.

Maybe one day,

laziness won't be such an easy option.

But until then,

cheers to this pen.

***Third Eye***

Confined cabins

and coffined classrooms

can numb down a part of you to death

and I've been doing nothing

but performing rituals of poetry

to keep it alive.

## *Self-Centered*

Consumed by cunningness,
blinded by brilliance,
lured by lordliness ,
we strive to reach the top
even if it means
stepping on other shoulders.

Maybe that is why
we find ourselves falling in
our dreams so often.

*Playing Pretend*

Tonight, I'll try again.
To close my eyes
as hard as I can
and try
to never wake up again.

Tonight,
I'll shut the lights to
pitch black
and make darkness
my new habitat.

I'll fight against my thoughts.
I'll try to suppress memories
to see if my lungs cease to breathe, to
see if my heart stops to beat.

***The Constant***

The children sob. Their
mothers sob. The parted
lovers sob. The
fortunate sob.
The penniless sob.
The old sob.
The virile sob.

But nobody learns.

Mohammed Adil

What is more apocalyptic
than a generation
that takes pride in its sins, a world
where angels cry and devils sing ?

***Bats***

Nothing, is more relatable to me
than a bat,
a creature that barely harms
but is feared by people.

An innocent beast
that meditates during the day
and finds refuge in
the night.

I've never understood
what harm, there is,
in just hanging by the braches of peace
while everyone wants to add
to a tree
of chaos and restlessness.

Mohammed Adil

*Ashes Don't Burn*

Set ablaze in flames and fumes,
the dying wood crackles and coughs;
but once, ash, it becomes,
it halts the struggle, it ceases to burn.

The ashes spurn the flames
as they've suffered enough
the same way
my weary heart spurns other hearts,
and can no longer love,
can no longer hurt. With
time, more numb,
these loving nerves have become.

To fall in love once more,
this abandoned heart, everyday yearns
but you know ashes do not matter

for ashes do not burn.

### ***Scratch The Skin Till You See Gold***

Cage my body,
pin my limbs
and rain upon me
your merciless sins.

Lash me hard with
the strongest cane you can find.
Show me that I'm human,
show me that it is in me to be kind.

Tell me that I'm more than numb. Tell me that there is more to this life than just being glum.

Mohammed Adil

***Can A Broken Heart Love Once More?***

A heart which used to be a virgin white cloth,
now dragged and disowned;
scraped over pricking and protruding thorns.

With a heart,
a life, with
little
or no hope;
with a body, breathing,
but almost comatose;
with lips that lament and,
all day, mourn;
I beg you to tell me if
a broken heart
can love once more?

***Typhoons And Treats***

Foolish trees dance
and celebrate the gentle breeze
only to be destroyed by
the storming winds.

The devastated branches
sprout new leaves
that again,
grow singing
to the teasing breeze.
The innocent leaves continue to
rejoice;
unaware,
of the nature's
violent deceit.

Mohammed Adil

***Eating His Children***

The ocean feels cherished
when tiny ships sail across
his skin,
when adrenaline-rich men
surf on his waves.
But what no one sees is
his pain
when people pierce
through his skin
and fish out his children with
sharp hooks and ropes and
sometimes,
kill the eldest one's
inside him.

Sins are the roses that lure us

into grabbing them,

making us forget

about the thorns that

may cut us

here

or

in the afterlife.

Mohammed Adil

What crime

has mother earth committed

to be drilled,

have her blood

sucked out

with giant machinery

and traded off

to feed

our greed

for wealth?

## WEEPING IN WORDS

### *War Of The Waters*

The cruel sea
sends its troops of waves
to break the rocks that
stand in its way.

Against the obstinate stones,
the furious tides crash and splash,
but the rocks do not move
nor do they mind
the everyday clash..

Never do they lose calm.
Never do they frown. Instead,
they laugh at the sea

and they taunt :
Come at us with all you have.

# Mohammed Adil

Charge at us like a raging hound.

Watch our might as we stand our ground.

Witness our courage as we never back down,

for it is not us,

but your cowardly waves

who bounce off us

making squeamish sounds.

## WEEPING IN WORDS

Your suffering

offers strength

after it moulds

just as

the night promises

a new dawn

after it has taken its course.

**Our Dying Souls**

When our dreams begin to die,
we wish again for them to be true.
Our aspiration refuses to hide.
Our optimism demands to rule.

The cycle of hopeless hope
rewrites.
Dreams are what keep our dying souls
alive.

Each man's mind
is a universe within itself,
far beyond anyone's understanding
but his own.
If you don't comprehend it,
you might as well be living
in someone else's head.

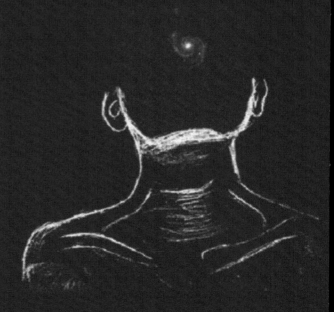

Made in the USA
Coppell, TX
29 November 2023